THE CHINESE HOROSCOPES LIBRARY

SNAKE

KWOK MAN-HO

DORLING KINDERSLEY
LONDON • NEW YORK • STUTTGART

A DORLING KINDERSLEY BOOK

Senior Editor   Sharon Lucas
Art Editor   Camilla Fox
Managing Editor   Krystyna Mayer
Managing Art Editor   Derek Coombes
DTP Designer   Doug Miller
Production Controller   Antony Heller
US Editor   Laaren Brown

Artworks: Danuta Mayer 4, 8, 11, 17, 27, 29, 31, 33, 35;
Giuliano Fornari 21; Jane Thomson; Sarah Ponder.

Special Photography by Steve Gorton. Thank you to the Bristol City Museum & Art Gallery,
Oriental Section; The British Museum, Chinese Post Office, and The Powell-Cotton Museum.

Additional Photography: Eric Crichton, Steve Gorton, Dave King, Diana Miller, Steve Shott,
Chris Stevens, Paul Williams.

Picture Credits: Bridgeman Art Library/Oriental Museum, Durham University 15, The
British Museum 23bl, Circa Photo Library 14.

First American Edition, 1994
2 4 6 8 10 9 7 5 3 1

Published in the United States by Dorling Kindersley Publishing, Inc., 95 Madison Avenue,
New York, New York 10016

ISBN 1-56458-610-3
Library of Congress Catalog Number 93-48006

Reproduced by GRB Editrice, Verona, Italy
Printed and bound in Hong Kong by Imago

CONTENTS

INTRODUCING CHINESE HOROSCOPES

For thousands of years, the Chinese have used their astrology and religion to establish a harmony between people and the world around them.

The exact origins of the twelve animals of Chinese astrology – the Rat, Ox, Tiger, Rabbit, Dragon, Snake, Horse, Ram, Monkey, Rooster, Dog, and Pig – remain a mystery. Nevertheless, these animals are important in Chinese astrology. They are much more than general signposts to the year and to the possible good or bad times ahead for us all. The twelve animals of Chinese astrology are considered to be a reflection of the Universe itself.

YIN AND YANG SYMBOL
White represents the female force of yin, and black represents the masculine force of yang.

YIN AND YANG
The many differences in our natures, moods, health, and fortunes reflect the wider changes within the Universe. The Chinese believe that

every single thing in the Universe is held in balance by the dynamic, cosmic forces of yin and yang. Yin is feminine, watery, and cool; the force of the Moon and the rain. Yang is masculine, solid, and hot; the force of the Sun and the Earth. According to ancient Chinese belief, the concentrated essences of yin and yang became the four seasons, and the scattered essences of yin and yang became the myriad creatures that are found on Earth.

The twelve animals of Chinese astrology are all associated with either yin or yang. The forces of yin rise as Winter approaches. These forces decline with the warmth of Spring, when yang begins to assert itself. Even in the course of a normal day, yin and yang are at work, constantly changing and balancing. These forces also naturally rise and fall within us all.

Everyone has their own internal balance of yin and yang. This affects our tempers, ambitions, and health. We also respond to the changes of weather, to the environment, and to the people who surround us.

THE FIVE ELEMENTS

All that we can touch, taste, or see is divided into five basic types or elements – wood, fire, earth, gold, and water. Everything in the Universe can be linked to one of these elements.

For example, the element fire is linked to the Snake and to the Horse. This element is also linked to the color red, bitter-tasting food, the season of Summer, and the emotion of joy. The activity of these elements indicates the fortune that may befall us.

AN INDIVIDUAL DISCOVERY

Chinese astrology can help you balance your yin and yang. It can also tell you which element you are, and the colors, tastes, parts of the body, or emotions that are linked to your particular sign. Your fortune can be prophesied according to the year, month, day, and hour in which you were born. You can identify the type of people to whom you are attracted, and the career that will suit your character. You can understand your changes of mood, your reactions to other places and to other people. In essence, you can start to discover what makes you an individual.

DIVINATION STICKS
Another ancient and popular method of Chinese fortune-telling is using special divination sticks to obtain a specific reading from prediction books.

CASTING YOUR HOROSCOPE

The Chinese calendar is based on the movement of the Moon, unlike the calendar used in the Western world, which is based on the movement of the Sun.

Before you begin to cast your Chinese horoscope, check your year of birth on the chart on pages 44 to 45. Check particularly carefully if you were born in the early months of the year. The Chinese year does not usually begin until January or February, and you might belong to the previous Chinese year. For example, if you were born in 1961 you might assume that you were born in the Year of the Ox. However, if your birthday falls before February 15 you belong to the previous Chinese year, which is the Year of the Rat.

THE SIXTY-YEAR CYCLE

The Chinese measure the passing of time by cycles of sixty years. The twelve astrological animals appear five times during the sixty-year cycle, and they appear in a slightly different form every time. For example, if you were born in 1953

you are a Snake on the Grass, but if you were born in 1965, you are a Snake Coming Out of the Hole.

MONTHS, DAYS, AND HOURS

The twelve lunar months of the Chinese calendar do not correspond exactly with the twelve Western calendar months. This is because Chinese months are lunar, whereas Western months are solar. Chinese months are normally twenty-nine to thirty days long, and every three to four years an extra month is added to keep approximately in step with the Western year.

One Chinese hour is equal to two Western hours, and the twelve Chinese hours correspond to the twelve animal signs.

The year, month, day, and hour of birth are the keys to Chinese astrology. Once you know them, you can start to unlock your personal Chinese horoscope.

Water

Earth   Gold

Wood   Yin

Fire   Yang

CHINESE ASTROLOGICAL WHEEL
*In the center of the wheel is the yin and
yang symbol. It is surrounded by the
Chinese astrological character linked to
each animal. The band of color indicates
your element, and the outer ring reveals
whether you are yin or yang.*

MYTHS AND LEGENDS

The Jade Emperor, heaven's ruler, asked to see the Earth's twelve
most interesting animals. When they arrived, he was impressed
by the Snake's sinuousness, and awarded it sixth place.

The Snake is a female symbol in China. It is respected for its great intelligence, but it is also regarded as treacherous. River gods were thought to be in snake form, and the Snake was often worshiped. Snake liver was regarded for its medicinal value, and it is believed that snakeskin should never be thrown away, because it will eventually bring wealth to the owner. Dreams of a black snake foretell the birth of a girl, dreams of a white or gray snake foretell the birth of a boy, and if a man dreams of a single snake it forecasts a new relationship with a woman.

SMILING SNAKE

This finely carved, ancient Chinese green jade snake shows the snake's scaly markings, as well as its typically secretive smile.

THE UNSUCCESSFUL SNAKE

Long ago, there was an unsuccessful snake. These creatures are usually harbingers of death for the Chinese, because they appear suddenly and kill swiftly. However, this particular snake was neither fast nor overly poisonous. Although he always tried his best, he did not frighten anyone. One day, a horse gave him a blow to the head, leaving him unable to bite or poison anything. The snake was bitterly disappointed, but refused to give up hope. "After all," he said to himself, "just seeing a snake can sometimes

TORTOISE AND SNAKE

A snake on top of a tortoise symbolizes the direction of the north. This figure is made of bronze and is from China's Han dynasty (206BC–AD220).

give humans a fatal heart attack." He moved to the Buddhist temple, but the old and the weak there did not pay him the slightest amount of attention, or show the merest flicker of fear, no matter how fierce or vicious he looked.

Downcast, he decided to throw himself to his death that night off the top of the pagoda. When all was quiet and dark, the snake slowly

climbed up the pagoda. He failed to notice a thief, weighed down with stolen temple treasures. Just as the the snake hurled himself suicidally from the top of the pagoda, the thief stopped. The snake fell straight onto the thief's neck.

The thief collapsed, uttering a blood-curdling scream. The snake was stunned, but he was the hero of the hour, and the temple monks could not reward him enough. They made a snake den in the temple, brought him tasty tidbits, and made his life as luxurious as possible. Unwittingly, the unsuccessful snake had found success at last.

· SNAKE ·
PERSONALITY

*The appearance and manner of the Snake are refined and
elegant. It is a polite and confident creature, and finds
itself attracted to debate and investigation.*

You tend to be found at the center of social events, holding court with your conversational skills and your humor. You enjoy the exchange of ideas, but can easily become bored.

MOTIVATION

You are a good judge of character and opportunities. When you have a target for yourself you will not abandon it until completion.

Usually you are patient and considerate, but if you find yourself under threat, you react sharply and are prepared to take revenge.

It is important that you achieve your goals with subtlety since you do not handle confrontation or failure easily. You are always prepared to give advice but find it hard to accept it when it is offered. When you have to ease yourself out of difficult situations, you will happily use all

ENTWINED SNAKE AND TORTOISE
The snake and tortoise on this 16th-century rubbing represent the struggle between yin and yang. On the tortoise's shell are the constellations of Heaven and the eight trigrams of the I Ching.

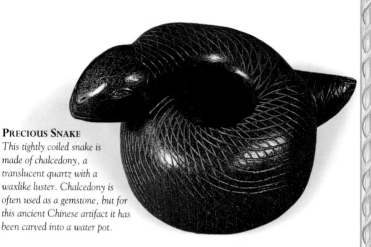

PRECIOUS SNAKE
This tightly coiled snake is made of chalcedony, a translucent quartz with a waxlike luster. Chalcedony is often used as a gemstone, but for this ancient Chinese artifact it has been carved into a water pot.

possible means. These methods and your constant quest for success and achievements can make you seem selfish and proud. However, once you feel that your problems have been resolved and your position is safe, you should become more tranquil and understanding.

THE INNER SNAKE
You are happiest when you are immersed deep in conversation, occasionally pausing for reflection, then continuing from a new angle. You are calm and peaceful, and your friendships tend to be extremely trusting and long-term.

There is a certain mystery and depth within you that others find attractive, and you are a sensual and passionate romantic partner.

You jealously guard the people who are close to you, and take great personal care of anything that you consider important. Consequently, as a parent you are protective, understanding, and always an effective communicator.

THE SNAKE CHILD
The young Snake requires plenty of tenderness and attention, and needs to avoid tense situations or arguments.

· SNAKE ·
LOVE

The Snake is seductive, passionate, and highly charismatic.
It guards its loved ones jealously and needs to be at the
center of its partner's life.

A combination of physical and mental attraction is very important in your emotional relationships. You love to exchange ideas and interests, and once you discover your romantic match, you are an amenable, humorous, and sensitive partner.

Although you guard your partner extremely jealously, you are also tempted to roam. Regardless of possible infidelities, however, you tend to cling to your committed relationship and are eager to keep your partner within your control. You enjoy attention and always like to please, but jealous scenes make you withdraw from the intensity of romance.

Ideally, you are suited to the Ox or the Rooster. The Ox will tolerate your selfishness and can provide you with comfort and security. The Rooster shares your interest in appearance, and you are both dependent on news, gossip, and meaningful conversations.

You are also well matched to the Rabbit, Ram, and Snake. You share the Rabbit's need

GODDESS OF LOVE
Kuan Yin is a powerful figure in Chinese mythology. Once a male Buddhist deity, she is now known as the goddess of mercy, and as Sung-tzu, the giver of children.

CHINESE COMPATIBILITY WHEEL

Find your animal sign, then look for the animals that share its background color – the Snake has a yellow background and is most compatible with the Rooster and the Ox. The symbol in the center of the wheel represents double happiness.

for a safe, comfortable environment, and it will allow you to feel that you are in control. You appreciate the Ram's creativity, but the relationship could easily become too disorganized. A relationship with another Snake could prove very powerful, but you may have to spend much time apart.

You share a great sense of respect with the Rat, but you both need to develop some

ORCHID
In China, the orchid, or Lan Hua, is an emblem of love and beauty. It is also a fertility symbol and represents many offspring.

tolerance; the friendly Dragon will admire your wisdom; and the Pig, despite its naïveté, will know how to cope with your complexities. You admire the Dog's honesty, and, if you assure it of your tenderness, it will give you the space you need.

A relationship with the Tiger or the Monkey is likely to be very difficult. The Tiger is too vivacious and you are too possessive, and although the Monkey shares your intelligence, it is too fickle and will refuse to be controlled.

· SNAKE ·
CAREER

The Snake makes the most of its career opportunities. It is ambitious and intelligent, but is content to relax when it has achieved its goals.

TEACHER
The Snake is wise and astute, and can easily turn the process of learning into an enjoyable experience. It is a charming creature and can inspire great loyalty, create a happy atmosphere, and express its ideas with strength and conviction. It is, therefore, a naturally gifted teacher. It also possesses the ability to learn from any mistakes that it might make.

Student's notebook

PSYCHOLOGIST
The field of psychology could be a rewarding arena for the Snake's highly developed personal skills. Juggling appeals to the Snake because it requires an extremely deep level of concentration.

Juggling balls

Building blocks

RESTAURATEUR

Owning and running a restaurant can be a very pleasant career for the Snake. It loves to indulge itself and has excellent taste. The Snake possesses many creative talents and would enjoy serving beautifully presented delicacies such as smoked salmon parcels and pearly pork balls.

Smoked salmon parcels

Pearly pork balls

PHILOSOPHER

This Chinese lacquer geomancy compass would be used by a Chinese philosopher for feng shui, the ancient method of divining the hidden energy in the landscape. Such esoteric arts interest the Snake profoundly.

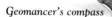

Geomancer's compass

Lawyer's briefcase

LAWYER

Conducting lawsuits and advising clients on their legal rights and obligations requires clarity of thought, a single-minded approach, and a willingness to seize opportunities. The Snake has all of these qualities and is rarely distracted from its professional aims.

HEALTH

Good health is dependent upon the balance of yin and yang in the body. Yin and yang are in a continual state of flux, but they always remain in harmony.

There is a natural minimum and maximum level of yin and yang in the human body. The body's energy is known as ch'i and is a yang force. The movement of ch'i in the human body is complemented by the movement of blood, which is a yin force. The very slightest displacement of the balance of yin or yang in the body can quickly lead to poor health. However,

LINGCHIH FUNGUS

The fungus shown in this detail from a Ch'ing dynasty bowl is the "immortal" lingchih fungus, which symbolizes longevity.

ANGELICA

This herb is widely used in Chinese medicine and is highly regarded for its success in the treament of gynecological disorders.

yang illness can be cured by yin treatment, and yin illness can be cured by yang treatment. Everybody has their own individual balance of yin and yang. It is likely that a hot-tempered person will have strong yang forces, and that a peaceful person will have strong yin forces. Your nature is identified with your health, and before Chinese medicine can be prescribed, your moods have to be carefully taken into account. A balance of joy, anger, sadness, happiness, worry, pensiveness, and fear must always be maintained. This fine balance is known in China as the Harmony of the Seven Sentiments.

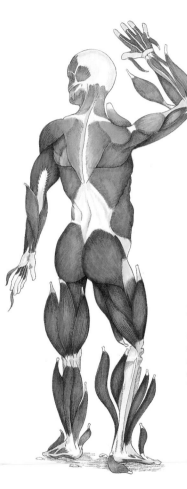

Born in the Year of the Snake, you
are associated with the element fire.
This element is linked with the heart,
small intestine, tongue, and pulse.
These are the parts of the body
that are relevant to the pattern of
your health. You are also
associated with the emotion of joy
and with bitter-tasting food.

Angelica (*Angelica archangelica*) is
associated with your Chinese
astrological sign. It is prescribed to
warm the spleen and stomach,
restore ch'i and blood, and renew
health and strength. In combination
with other herbs, angelica is used to
treat poor circulation, breathing
difficulties, and rheumatoid arthritis.
Angelica is also one of the ingredients
of the Soup to Mend Yang and
Restore the Elements, which treats
partial paralysis.

Chinese medicine is highly
specific; therefore, never take
angelica or any other herb unless you
are following professional advice
from a fully qualified Chinese or
Western doctor.

ASTROLOGY AND ANATOMY

*Your element, fire, is associated with the
heart and the small intestine. The heart
is a yin organ, and the small intestine
is a yang organ.*

· SNAKE ·
LEISURE

The Snake prefers creative hobbies to active pastimes. It likes to indulge itself with life's luxuries, but will happily spend time talking, reading, or playing music.

Crystal ball

Chinese jade plaque

THE MYSTIC ARTS
Communication is one of the Snake's greatest pleasures, to the extent that it might even try to make contact with other worlds. The Snake has good taste and would appreciate the simple mystery of this crystal ball and the visual splendor of these Chinese tarot cards.

Chinese tarot cards

ASTROLOGY
The Snake is linked with astrology on this ancient plaque, which shows snakes and astronomical constellations.

SWIMMING

Goggles

The Snake likes to be fit, but tends to avoid vigorous physical exercise. Swimming, however, does have appeal, because it can be done alone and at the Snake's own pace. It is an excellent form of exercise for posture and breathing, and intensifies the Snake's elegance and peaceful aura.

Swimming caps

Trunks

ANTIQUES

The Snake is excited when it can acquire unusual objects, such as this Ch'ing dynasty bowl, which has been lovingly restored with gold to its former glory.

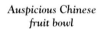

Auspicious Chinese fruit bowl

Archaeological tools

ARCHAEOLOGY

The field of archaeology is an intriguing and rewarding one for the Snake. It is meticulous and will painstakingly search for exotic artifacts.

Hand picks

· SNAKE ·
SYMBOLISM

Each astrological animal is linked with a certain food, direction, color, emotion, association, and symbol. The Snake is also associated with the season of Summer.

COLOR
Every Chinese New Year, small red envelopes of money are handed out to children, because red is the color of long life and good fortune. It is also the color that is associated with the Snake.

Chinese chop print with snake

FOOD
There are five tastes according to Chinese astrology – salty, acrid, bitter, sweet, and sour. Bitter foods, such as chicory, are linked with the Snake.

Chicory

Antique Chinese compass

Hand grenades

DIRECTION
The Chinese compass points south, whereas the Western compass points north. The Snake's direction is the south.

ASSOCIATION
All forms of warfare are linked with the Snake.

Weights and spring balance

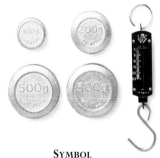

Joyful baby

SYMBOL
Weights and measures are the Snake's symbols in Chinese astrology.

EMOTION
Joy is the emotion that is connected with the Snake.

SNAKE COMING OUT OF THE HOLE

~ 1905 1965 ~

This Snake is unsure where it is going. You are associated with a bud about to break into flower, suggesting that you are on the verge of doing something.

Although you have many of the Snake's skills and attributes, sometimes you are not quite as successful as the other types of Snake. This may be because you are never quite sure what is happening.

PERSONALITY

You are likely to be popular and to be highly respected for your trustworthiness. However, the public acclaim that others seem to receive with no effort at all could seem to pass you by. This can be frustrating, but do not allow it to become embittering.

Try to remain open, cheerful, and generous. This should always stand you in good stead, even if you sometimes feel undervalued.

The investigative aspect of the Snake is heightened in the Snake Coming Out of the Hole. You probably find it difficult, if not impossible, to relinquish any issues that you feel strongly about.

This may, in part, explain why you are never likely to receive the amount of praise that you expect. You tend toward obsession, when a little distance and objectivity might prove more beneficial and impressive to other people.

No one is ever likely to doubt your sincerity, but they cannot always stay with you while you pursue an issue to the bitter end. Sometimes your obsessions can make you unsettling to live with.

FEMALE CHARACTERISTICS

Because of the calming and soothing yin influence, the female Snake Coming Out of the Hole tends to be less frustrated than the male. Considerable fame can often be

Snake Coming Out of the Hole

achieved by the female, although it is invariably ephemeral and should never be taken for granted.

RELATIONSHIPS

In all your personal relationships, whether with your partner or your family, try to learn to give and take more. It is probably advisable for you to have children slightly later in life. This should reduce the risks of any personality clashes, and a little maturity may be just as helpful to you as to your children.

PROSPECTS

Always pursue the ideals and the issues that interest you, for it is through your drive that they will be properly addressed. Do not expect to be praised for your hard work, however. Others will invariably receive the credit, but if you really care about an issue this should not trouble you unduly. Your main concerns are with justice and doing what is right. Remember this, and be comforted when your life seems fraught with frustration.

SNAKE IN THE FISH POND

~ 1917 1977 ~

*Some Snakes feel comfortable in the water, but most do not.
You may be out of your element, but you are also stubborn,
for you are associated with a tough nail.*

You are unlikely ever to give up – you know your position in life and accept that this is where you will stay. You will invariably try your best to make the most of it.

Life is often not easy for you, but even though you may not be doing exactly what you want to do, you are always likely to retain your innate obstinacy. This personality trait is often a strength because you rarely allow things to overcome you, but the struggle can sometimes be exhausting, too.

YOUTH
The early part of your life is likely to be fraught with struggle, but try not to give in to your anger and frustration. Always remember the image of the nail – you are personally strong and can withstand a good "hammering," but try not to be too tough and obstructive.

CAREER
Luckily, all your efforts do not go unobserved. Your determination is noted by those in authority, and you are recognized as a person of integrity and value.

FRIENDSHIPS
Your obstinacy is likely to cause you some problems. Consequently, it is a good idea for you to develop the Snake characteristic of making good, long-term friends, who can offer you valuable affection and support.

FAMILY
If you are an eldest child, you will probably find that life is easier than if you are a second or third child. The Snake in the Fish Pond as an eldest child seems to be far more comfortable in its element, and is able to progress much further in life as a result.

Snake in the Fish Pond

RELATIONSHIPS

A committed relationship is likely to be good for you, as long as you choose a partner who is your equal. You may find that you often clash with your partner, but do not lose heart, because real affection and a mature relationship should eventually ensue.

CHILDREN

If left unchecked, your strong and forceful personality may leave little room for your children to develop. Try to encourage them in their own interests, even if these are not necessarily yours. Be generous, and allow them the personal space to be different from you.

PROSPEROUS SNAKE

~ 1929 1989 ~

*All the best, most successful qualities of the Snake are
magnified in you. Even your name suggests that you will
always enjoy extremely good fortune.*

Y ou are associated with blossoming
and succeeding, which adds to the
overall sense of auspiciousness that
invariably surrounds you.

PERSONALITY

You tend to be very active and
occupied. You enjoy a full social life
and become bored if there is nothing
to excite or interest you.

Other people might be frustrated
by a lack of stimulus, but you cope
with it by becoming active.
Invariably, your action leads to
success in many different areas.

You have a very attractive
personality and may even become
famous. Everything you do tends to
turn out well, and sometimes
spectacularly so. People turn to you
when they want to be stimulated into
thinking or acting differently. This
brings you great personal
satisfaction, and a good income.

FEMALE CHARACTERISTICS

Because of the yin influence, the
female Prosperous Snake may
sometimes suffer – her innovation
and love of risk may be mistrusted by
others. This should change over
time, but will probably affect her
early years. As an eventually
successful Snake woman, she can
change public prejudices, but it may
be at some personal cost.

FRIENDSHIPS

All Snakes are compassionate
creatures, and it is advisable for you
to keep this sense of compassion
running alongside your success
stories. If you start bragging or
boasting, rather than doing and
achieving, you may find that your
friends and peers turn away from
you. Always remember to be kind
and considerate, for you can easily
afford to do so.

Prosperous Snake

PROSPECTS

Try to control your inclination toward avarice. It is a petty trait, and one that is unworthy of you. If you concentrate on the job at hand, and continue to do it well, you should easily earn the rewards that you deserve. Always remember that if you give in to temptation and push too hard for material benefit and personal advantage, you may suffer as a consequence. If you go down unsuitable pathways and abuse your considerable skills, intellect, and good fortune, this would be a great shame. Although you might be better off financially, it would be at the expense of your integrity.

SNAKE SLEEPING IN THE WINTER

~ 1941 2001 ~

To sleep happily throughout the Winter, this Snake must take in an adequate amount of food to sustain itself. Symbolically, for this Snake, food corresponds to success.

It is very important for you to be a success. Luckily, as a Snake, success is invariably yours. You must be careful, though, for you are linked to the dead of Winter, emphasizing Winter's bitterness and pain.

This could mean that although you may be successful, you could also be building future problems for yourself. Do not worry too much, for if you heed this warning, you should be able to enjoy the benefits of life while avoiding the pitfalls.

PERSONALITY

You have a confusing, changeable personality. If you decide to direct all your energies toward achieving material success, you may find yourself concentrating on one side of your personality. Alternatively, if you moderate this tendency, you can probably develop another side of

yourself. At times you may oscillate between these facets of yourself – try to be consistent, for this behavior is invariably bewildering to others.

By nature you are hardworking, very ambitious, and careful with money. In moderation, these are all admirable qualities, but try not to overwork, for this could destroy valuable relationships.

Try to keep your ambition under firm control, for this could lead you into actions of which you will later be ashamed. Even worse, these actions could also leave you with formidable enemies.

In financial matters, by all means exercise a small degree of thrift, but do not allow this to develop into a form of meanness.

Do your best to enjoy life, and remember to give yourself a treat sometimes, rather than always

Snake Sleeping in the Winter

looking to save. Try to value yourself, and your friendships and relationships, as much as, or even more than, money and success.

CAREER

At work, people in authority will probably value you as a hardworking person and will assist your career. Beware that you do not use this influence and power to harm others, however, and make sure that you do not make your way to the top by abusing your peers.

RELATIONSHIPS

Because of the yang influence, the male Snake Sleeping in the Winter in particular needs to find an older partner. Both males and females should try to find someone older, however, to help keep their strong personalities under control.

You should enjoy a happy and rewarding partnership, but may be tempted to flirt with other people. Always try to curb these unfaithful impulses, for you will invariably hurt others, as well as yourself.

SNAKE ON THE GRASS

~ 1953 2013 ~

Restless, always wanting to go to faraway places, desperate to start new projects, and do yet more — this is the dynamic Snake on the Grass.

You are full of energy and are very clever, but this does not always lead to an easy life. It is beneficial for you to pay considerable attention to your relationship with your elders, for you are linked to ancestor worship – keeping the dead happy.

FEMALE CHARACTERISTICS

Because of the influence of the yin force, it is important for the female Snake on the Grass to pay proper attention to people in authority.

CAREER

You may find it unfair and ultimately frustrating that wealth and fame do not come straight away. To be successful, you will probably have to work very hard indeed. Always try to retain a sensible and objective outlook, and do not allow yourself to become obsessed with the pursuit of wealth and status.

The natural enthusiasm and energy that you bring to any task that interests you, and your obvious intelligence, will soon earn you the admiration of others. You may find that someone in authority begins to look after you, and furthers your career. In the future you will probably have to break free from this liaison, but it should be of great value to you at the time.

FAMILY

In your youth, you probably had a stormy relationship with your family. Perhaps they did not understand your drive, and you did not understand their caution.

You may even have considered them to be irritating, and less intelligent than you. Both you and your family will simply have to learn that the passing of time can bring a renewal of relationships.

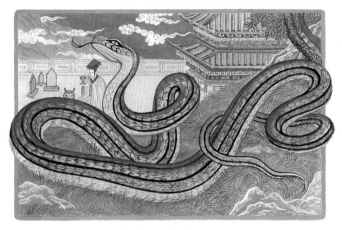

Snake on the Grass

Your family problems will not affect your ability to form very good relationships with your partner and your children, and you should gradually be able to re-establish family links.

RELATIONSHIPS

Because you are a vivacious Snake, you are particularly prone to being flirtatious, or even unfaithful. This can be a rather disruptive tendency, so make every effort to choose a partner who can balance your energy and drive with a sense of calm and a long-term perspective.

Learn to appreciate your partner's gentle, calming influence, and do not run off to others just because they seem to be more attractive. If you concentrate on learning to live with your partner, you are likely to be happy and successful.

PROSPECTS

Financial success is likely to come later in life, but luckily, you are not overly motivated by monetary gain. Instead you enjoy the stimulation of fresh challenges, and prefer to use your intelligence and skills to encounter new ideas.

YOUR CHINESE
MONTH OF BIRTH

*Find the table with your year of birth, and see where your
birthday falls. For example, if you were born on
August 30, 1953, you were born in Chinese month 7.*

1 You must learn to relax and to say what you feel. Do not always let other people set life's agenda.

2 You can be calm and cool, but you can also blaze up. Try to keep your temper under control.

3 You always appear to be in control, but are invariably anxious. Be truthful in your self-expression.

4 You are extremely enthusiastic. Your career will be very successful if you are your own boss.

5 You are considerate, but can be mean. Sometimes you make people uncomfortable by judging them.

6 You are very well balanced. You are capable, a pleasant colleague, and excellent company.

7 You are well liked, despite the odd disagreement. Learn to listen more, and never give up.

8 You have a good sense of humor. Although you will take charge, you prefer to work by general agreement.

9 You are determined to succeed and refuse to be deterred. Spend more time building friendships.

10 You are popular and successful, and a figure in authority should help you to prosper.

11 Your feelings can overwhelm you and swamp your judgment. Try to be more thoughtful.

12 You express your feelings honestly. You are adaptable and should succeed in any situation.

* Some Chinese years contain double months:	
1917: Month 2	1941: Month 6
Feb 22 – March 22	June 25 – July 23
March 23 – April 20	July 24 – Aug 22
2001: Month 4	
April 23 – May 22	
May 23 – June 20	

1905	
Feb 4 – March 5	1
March 6 – April 4	2
April 5 – May 3	3
May 4 – June 2	4
June 3 – July 2	5
July 3 – July 31	6
Aug 1 – Aug 29	7
Aug 30 – Sept 28	8
Sept 29 – Oct 27	9
Oct 28 – Nov 26	10
Nov 27 – Dec 25	11
Dec 26 – Jan 24 1906	12

1917	
Jan 23 – Feb 21	1
See double months box	2
April 21 – May 20	3
May 21 – June 18	4
June 19 – July 18	5
July 19 – Aug 17	6
Aug 18 – Sept 15	7
Sept 16 – Oct 15	8
Oct 16 – Nov 14	9
Nov 15 – Dec 13	10
Dec 14 – Jan 12 1918	11
Jan 13 – Feb 10	12

1929	
Feb 10 – March 10	1
March 11 – April 18	2
April 19 – May 8	3
May 9 – June 6	4
June 7 – July 6	5
July 7 – Aug 4	6
Aug 5 – Sept 2	7
Sept 3 – Oct 2	8
Oct 3 – Oct 30	9
Nov 1 – Nov 30	10
Dec 1 – Dec 30	11
Dec 31 – Jan 29 1930	12

1941	
Jan 27 – Feb 25	1
Feb 26 – March 27	2
March 28 – April 25	3
April 26 – May 25	4
May 26 – June 24	5
See double months box	6
Aug 23 – Sept 20	7
Sept 21 – Oct 19	8
Oct 20 – Nov 18	9
Nov 19 – Dec 17	10
Dec 18 – Jan 16 1942	11
Jan 17 – Feb 14	12

1953	
Feb 14 – March 14	1
March 15 – April 13	2
April 14 – May 12	3
May 13 – June 10	4
June 11 – July 10	5
July 11 – Aug 8	6
Aug 9 – Sept 7	7
Sept 8 – Oct 7	8
Oct 8 – Nov 6	9
Nov 7 – Dec 5	10
Dec 6 – Jan 4 1954	11
Jan 5 – Feb 2	12

1965	
Feb 2 – March 2	1
March 3 – April 1	2
April 2 – April 30	3
May 1 – May 30	4
May 31 – June 28	5
June 29 – July 27	6
July 28 – Aug 26	7
Aug 27 – Sept 24	8
Sept 25 – Oct 23	9
Oct 24 – Nov 22	10
Nov 23 – Dec 22	11
Dec 23 – Jan 20 1966	12

1977	
Feb 18 – March 19	1
March 20 – April 17	2
April 18 – May 17	3
May 18 – June 16	4
June 17 – July 15	5
July 16 – Aug 14	6
Aug 15 – Sept 12	7
Sept 13 – Oct 12	8
Oct 13 – Nov 10	9
Nov 11 – Dec 10	10
Dec 11 – Jan 8 1978	11
Jan 9 – Feb 6	12

1989	
Feb 6 – March 7	1
March 8 – April 5	2
April 6 – May 4	3
May 5 – June 3	4
June 4 – July 2	5
July 3 – July 31	6
Aug 1 – Aug 30	7
Aug 31 – Sept 29	8
Sept 30 – Oct 28	9
Oct 29 – Nov 27	10
Nov 28 – Dec 27	11
Dec 28 – Jan 26 1990	12

2001	
Jan 24 – Feb 22	1
Feb 23 – March 24	2
March 25 – April 22	3
See double months box	4
June 21 – July 20	5
July 21 – Aug 18	6
Aug 19 – Sept 16	7
Sept 17 – Oct 16	8
Oct 17 – Nov 14	9
Nov 15 – Dec 14	10
Dec 15 – Jan 12 2002	11
Jan 13 – Feb 11	12

YOUR CHINESE DAY OF BIRTH

Refer to the previous page to discover the beginning of your Chinese month of birth, then use the chart below to calculate your Chinese day of birth.

If you were born on 5 May 1905, your birthday is in the Chinese month starting on 4 May. Find 4 on the chart below. Using 4 as the first day, count the days until you reach the date of your birthday. Remember that not all months contain 31 days. You were born on day 2 of the Chinese month.

If you were born in a Chinese double month, simply count the days from the first date of the month that contains your birthday.

1	2	3	4	5	6	7
8	9	10	11	12	13	14
15	16	17	18	19	20	21
22	23	24	25	26	27	28
29	30	31				

DAY 1, 10, 19, OR 28
You are trustworthy, and set high standards, but tend to rush your projects. Try to be cautious, and do not be too self-obsessed. You may receive unexpected money, but must control your spending. You are suited to a career in the public sector or the arts.

DAY 2, 11, 20, OR 29
You are honest and popular. You need peace, but also require lively company. You are prone to outbursts of temper. You tend to enjoy life, and make the most of your opportunities. You are suited to a literary or artistic career.

DAY 3, 12, 21, OR 30
You are quick-witted, but may appear to be difficult. As a result, people may be wary of being your friend. You have a disciplined character, and fight for the truth. You are suited to careers that have a competitive element.

Day 4, 13, 22, or 31

You are very warmhearted, but also have a reserved attitude, which can sometimes make you appear unapproachable. If you try to be more outgoing and sociable, you should become more popular. You have a calm and patient manner, and are suited to a career as an academic or a researcher.

Day 5, 14, or 23

Your fiery, obstinate nature can sometimes make it difficult for you to accept suggestions or opinions from others, and your stubbornness may lead to quarrels or problems. You should be lucky with money, and may often use your profits to set up new projects. Your innate intelligence will enable you to cope with a demanding career.

Day 6, 15, or 24

You have an open, stable, and cheerful character, and enjoy an active social life. You are affectionate and emotional, and have a tendency to daydream. This can lead to confusion, and your eagerness to help others may be stifled by your indecision. Although you will never be wealthy, you should always have enough money.

Day 7, 16, or 25

You enjoy a certain amount of excitement in your life, but must learn to become more realistic and disciplined. Although you are a natural performer, you should beware of alienating your friends or colleagues. In your career, the opportunity to travel is more important to you than a good salary or a high standard of living.

Day 8, 17, or 26

You have good judgement, but should not act too quickly. Your social skills may sometimes be lacking, and you may alienate other people, so try to be more tactful. You will experience poverty, but also wealth. Your calm and determined nature is combined with a free spirit, making you best suited to self-employment.

Day 9, 18, or 27

You are happy, optimistic, and warmhearted. You keep yourself busy, and are rarely troubled by trivialities. Occasionally you quarrel unnecessarily with your friends, and it is important for you to learn to control your moods. You are particularly suited to a career as a sole director or proprietor.

YOUR CHINESE
HOUR OF BIRTH

*In Chinese time, one hour is equal to two Western hours.
Each Chinese double hour is associated with one of the
twelve astrological animals.*

11 P.M. – 1 A.M. RAT HOUR
You are independent and have
a hot temper. Try to think before
you speak. Your thrifty nature will
be useful in business and at home.
You are willing to help those who
are close to you, and they will return
your support.

1 – 3 A.M. OX HOUR
Up to the age of twenty, your
life could be difficult, but your
fortunes are likely to improve after
these troublesome years. In your
career, be prepared to take a risk or
to leave home during your youth to
achieve your goals. You should enjoy
a prosperous old age.

3 – 5 A.M. TIGER HOUR
You have a lively and creative
nature, which may cause family
arguments in your youth. Between
the ages of twenty and forty you may
have many problems. Luckily, your
fortunes are likely to improve
dramatically in your forties.

5 – 7 A.M. RABBIT HOUR
Your parents should be
helpful, but your siblings may be
your rivals. You may have to move
away from home to achieve your full
potential at work. Your committed
relationship may take time to
become settled, but you should get
along much better with everyone
after middle age.

7 – 9 A.M. DRAGON HOUR
You have a quick-witted,
determined, and attractive nature.
Your life will be busy, but you could
sometimes be lonely. You should
achieve a good standard of living.
Try to curb your excessive self-
confidence, for it could make
working relationships difficult.

9 – 11 A.M. SNAKE HOUR
You have a talent for business and should find it easy to build your career and provide for your family. You have a very generous spirit and will gladly help your friends when they are in trouble. Unfortunately, family relationships are unlikely to run smoothly.

11 A.M. – 1 P.M. HORSE HOUR
You are active, clever, and obstinate. Try to listen to advice. You are fascinated with travel and with changing your life. Learn to control your extravagance, for it could lead to financial suffering.

1 – 3 P.M. RAM HOUR
Steady relationships with your family, friends, or partners are difficult, because you have an active nature. You are clever, but must not force your views on others. Your fortunes will be at their lowest in your middle age.

3 – 5 P.M. MONKEY HOUR
You earn and spend money easily. Your character is attractive, but frustrating, too. Sometimes your parents are not able to give you adequate moral support. Your committed relationship should be good, but do not brood over emotional problems for too long – if you do your career could suffer.

5 – 7 P.M. ROOSTER HOUR
In your teenage years you may have many arguments with your family. There could even be a family division, which should eventually be resolved. You are trustworthy, kind, and warmhearted, and never intend to hurt other people.

7 – 9 P.M. DOG HOUR
Your brave, capable, hard-working nature is ideally suited to self-employment, and the forecast for your career is excellent. Try to control your impatience and vanity. The quality of your life is far more important to you than the amount of money you have saved.

9 – 11 P.M. PIG HOUR
You are particularly skilled at manual work and always set yourself high standards. Although you are warmhearted, you do not like to surround yourself with too many friends. However, the people who are close to you have your complete trust. You can be easily upset by others, but are able to forgive and forget quickly.

YOUR FORTUNE IN OTHER ANIMAL YEARS

The Snake's fortunes fluctuate during the twelve animal years. It is best to concentrate on a year's positive aspects, and to take care when faced with the seemingly negative.

YEAR OF THE RAT
Your emotional affairs will go smoothly, and you should do well in your career. You may have minor money worries, but because the Year of the Rat is a good year for you, your happiness should more than compensate for these trivialities.

YEAR OF THE OX
This year is not an auspicious time to make investments, attempt to change career, or set up a new business. Be content to leave risk and speculation to other people, and concentrate on what is familiar, realistic, and available.

YEAR OF THE TIGER
Your fortunes will be mixed in the Year of the Tiger. The beginning of the year is likely to be marked with arguments and disagreements, but these are only temporary. The year should end on a happy note.

YEAR OF THE RABBIT
Disasters may seem to be confronting you in all areas of your life in the Year of the Rabbit. However, your family will provide you with an excellent place of refuge. Keep a low profile, wait patiently, and inevitably your life will improve.

YEAR OF THE DRAGON
You are susceptible to other people's lies and deceitfulness during the Year of the Dragon. As a result, your family life could become tense, strained, and difficult. Try to ignore idle gossip at all times, and do not allow it to make you feel stressed.

YEAR OF THE SNAKE
There could be many irritating difficulties for you in the Year of the Snake. However, if you remain on your guard, and choose your friends and partners wisely, you have a very good chance of being able to avoid these potential problems.

 YEAR OF THE HORSE
Serious change is likely to be forced upon you through the combination of ill-health and various financial difficulties. As a result, you may find yourself abroad, perhaps escaping from your problems, or even in search of work.

 YEAR OF THE RAM
Unfortunately, nothing seems to go well for you in the Year of the Ram. You are likely to have increasing difficulties in your family life and your professional life. It is best for you to be quiet and patient, and to simply wait for happier times.

 YEAR OF THE MONKEY
To start with, it may seem as if this year is just as difficult as the last, because you are likely to be encountering many of the same problems. However, as the year proceeds, your fortune will change, and you should enjoy some success.

 YEAR OF THE ROOSTER
This will be a good year for your family life and your professional life. Although you may encounter a few problems, they should not detract from the great opportunities that are soon to be revealed.

 YEAR OF THE DOG
Emotional affairs and travel are surrounded with particularly good fortune in the Year of the Dog. There is a strong possibility that some form of illness will cause you problems this year, so try to take care of your physical and mental health.

 YEAR OF THE PIG
You will enjoy many financial rewards this year. Unfortunately, there is a price to pay for this success, which could be in the form of deteriorating personal relationships. Avoid this at all costs by proceeding with caution.

YOUR CHINESE YEAR OF BIRTH

Your astrological animal corresponds to the Chinese year of your birth. It is the single most important key in the quest to unlock your Chinese horoscope.

Find your Western year of birth in the left-hand column of the chart. Your Chinese astrological animal is on the same line as your year of birth in the right-hand column of the chart. If you were born in the beginning of the year, check the middle column of the chart carefully. For example, if you were born in 1966, you might assume that you belong to the Year of the Horse. However, if your birthday falls before January 21, you actually belong to the Year of the Snake.

1900	Jan 31 – Feb 18, 1901	Rat
1901	Feb 19 – Feb 7, 1902	Ox
1902	Feb 8 – Jan 28, 1903	Tiger
1903	Jan 29 – Feb 15, 1904	Rabbit
1904	Feb 16 – Feb 3, 1905	Dragon
1905	Feb 4 – Jan 24, 1906	Snake
1906	Jan 25 – Feb 12, 1907	Horse
1907	Feb 13 – Feb 1, 1908	Ram
1908	Feb 2 – Jan 21, 1909	Monkey
1909	Jan 22 – Feb 9, 1910	Rooster
1910	Feb 10 – Jan 29, 1911	Dog
1911	Jan 30 – Feb 17, 1912	Pig
1912	Feb 18 – Feb 5, 1913	Rat
1913	Feb 6 – Jan 25, 1914	Ox
1914	Jan 26 – Feb 13, 1915	Tiger
1915	Feb 14 – Feb 2, 1916	Rabbit
1916	Feb 3 – Jan 22, 1917	Dragon

1917	Jan 23 – Feb 10, 1918	Snake
1918	Feb 11 – Jan 31, 1919	Horse
1919	Feb 1 – Feb 19, 1920	Ram
1920	Feb 20 – Feb 7, 1921	Monkey
1921	Feb 8 – Jan 27, 1922	Rooster
1922	Jan 28 – Feb 15, 1923	Dog
1923	Feb 16 – Feb 4, 1924	Pig
1924	Feb 5 – Jan 23, 1925	Rat
1925	Jan 24 – Feb 12, 1926	Ox
1926	Feb 13 – Feb 1, 1927	Tiger
1927	Feb 2 – Jan 22, 1928	Rabbit
1928	Jan 23 – Feb 9, 1929	Dragon
1929	Feb 10 – Jan 29, 1930	Snake
1930	Jan 30 – Feb 16, 1931	Horse
1931	Feb 17 – Feb 5, 1932	Ram
1932	Feb 6 – Jan 25, 1933	Monkey
1933	Jan 26 – Feb 13, 1934	Rooster

1934	Feb 14 – Feb 3, 1935	Dog	1971	Jan 27 – Feb 14, 1972	Pig
1935	Feb 4 – Jan 23, 1936	Pig	1972	Feb 15 – Feb 2, 1973	Rat
1936	Jan 24 – Feb 10, 1937	Rat	1973	Feb 3 – Jan 22, 1974	Ox
1937	Feb 11 – Jan 30, 1938	Ox	1974	Jan 23 – Feb 10, 1975	Tiger
1938	Jan 31 – Feb 18, 1939	Tiger	1975	Feb 11 – Jan 30, 1976	Rabbit
1939	Feb 19 – Feb 7, 1940	Rabbit	1976	Jan 31 – Feb 17, 1977	Dragon
1940	Feb 8 – Jan 26, 1941	Dragon	1977	Feb 18 – Feb 6, 1978	Snake
1941	Jan 27 – Feb 14, 1942	Snake	1978	Feb 7 – Jan 27, 1979	Horse
1942	Feb 15 – Feb 4, 1943	Horse	1979	Jan 28 – Feb 15, 1980	Ram
1943	Feb 5 – Jan 24, 1944	Ram	1980	Feb 16 – Feb 4, 1981	Monkey
1944	Jan 25 – Feb 12, 1945	Monkey	1981	Feb 5 – Jan 24, 1982	Rooster
1945	Feb 13 – Feb 1, 1946	Rooster	1982	Jan 25 – Feb 12, 1983	Dog
1946	Feb 2 – Jan 21, 1947	Dog	1983	Feb 13 – Feb 1, 1984	Pig
1947	Jan 22 – Feb 9, 1948	Pig	1984	Feb 2 – Feb 19, 1985	Rat
1948	Feb 10 – Jan 28, 1949	Rat	1985	Feb 20 – Feb 8, 1986	Ox
1949	Jan 29 – Feb 16, 1950	Ox	1986	Feb 9 – Jan 28, 1987	Tiger
1950	Feb 17 – Feb 5, 1951	Tiger	1987	Jan 29 – Feb 16, 1988	Rabbit
1951	Feb 6 – Jan 26, 1952	Rabbit	1988	Feb 17 – Feb 5, 1989	Dragon
1952	Jan 27 – Feb 13, 1953	Dragon	1989	Feb 6 – Jan 26, 1990	Snake
1953	Feb 14 – Feb 2, 1954	Snake	1990	Jan 27 – Feb 14, 1991	Horse
1954	Feb 3 – Jan 23, 1955	Horse	1991	Feb 15 – Feb 3, 1992	Ram
1955	Jan 24 – Feb 11, 1956	Ram	1992	Feb 4 – Jan 22, 1993	Monkey
1956	Feb 12 – Jan 30, 1957	Monkey	1993	Jan 23 – Feb 9, 1994	Rooster
1957	Jan 31 – Feb 17, 1958	Rooster	1994	Feb 10 – Jan 30, 1995	Dog
1958	Feb 18 – Feb 7, 1959	Dog	1995	Jan 31 – Feb 18, 1996	Pig
1959	Feb 8 – Jan 27, 1960	Pig	1996	Feb 19 – Feb 6, 1997	Rat
1960	Jan 28 – Feb 14, 1961	Rat	1997	Feb 7 – Jan 27, 1998	Ox
1961	Feb 15 – Feb 4, 1962	Ox	1998	Jan 28 – Feb 15, 1999	Tiger
1962	Feb 5 – Jan 24, 1963	Tiger	1999	Feb 16 – Feb 4, 2000	Rabbit
1963	Jan 25 – Feb 12, 1964	Rabbit	2000	Feb 5 – Jan 23, 2001	Dragon
1964	Feb 13 – Feb 1, 1965	Dragon	2001	Jan 24 – Feb 11, 2002	Snake
1965	Feb 2 – Jan 20, 1966	Snake	2002	Feb 12 – Jan 31, 2003	Horse
1966	Jan 21 – Feb 8, 1967	Horse	2003	Feb 1 – Jan 21, 2004	Ram
1967	Feb 9 – Jan 29, 1968	Ram	2004	Jan 22 – Feb 8, 2005	Monkey
1968	Jan 30 – Feb 16, 1969	Monkey	2005	Feb 9 – Jan 28, 2006	Rooster
1969	Feb 17 – Feb 5, 1970	Rooster	2006	Jan 29 – Feb 17, 2007	Dog
1970	Feb 6 – Jan 26, 1971	Dog	2007	Feb 18 – Feb 6, 2008	Pig